LEARN TO DRAW

DISNEY · PIXAR

COCO

Illustrated by the Disney Storybook Artists

Illustrated by the Disney Storybook Artists.

Published by Walter Foster Jr.,
an imprint of The Quarto Group.
6 Orchard Road, Suite 100, Lake Forest, CA 92630
www.QuartoKnows.com

Printed in China
10 9 8 7 6 5 4 3 2 1

MIX
Paper from
responsible sources
FSC® C017606
FSC
www.fsc.org

Table of Contents

Tools & Materials

You only need to gather a few simple art supplies before you begin. Start with a drawing pencil and an eraser. Make sure you also have a pencil sharpener and a ruler. To add color to your drawings, use markers, colored pencils, crayons, watercolors, or acrylic paint. The choice is yours!

drawing pencil
and paper

eraser

sharpener

colored pencils

felt-tip markers

paintbrushes
and paints

How to Use This Book

You can draw any of the characters in this book by following these simple steps.

First draw basic shapes using light lines that will be easy to erase.

Each new step is shown in blue, so you'll always know what to draw next.

Take your time and copy the blue lines, adding detail.

Darken the lines you want to keep and erase the rest.

Add color to your drawing with colored pencils, markers, paints, or crayons!

Miguel

Miguel Rivera is a 12-year-old boy who lives in the small Mexican town of Santa Cecilia. Born into a family of shoemakers, Miguel is torn because he doesn't really want to make shoes—he dreams of being a musician like his idol, Ernesto De La Cruz. But music has been forbidden in the Rivera household due to a generations-old family ban.

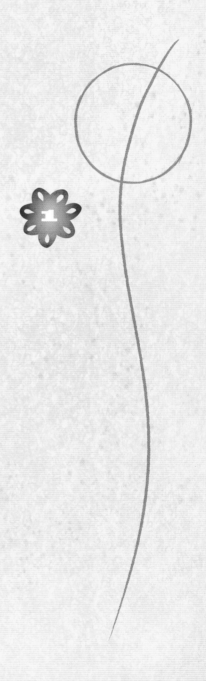

1

2

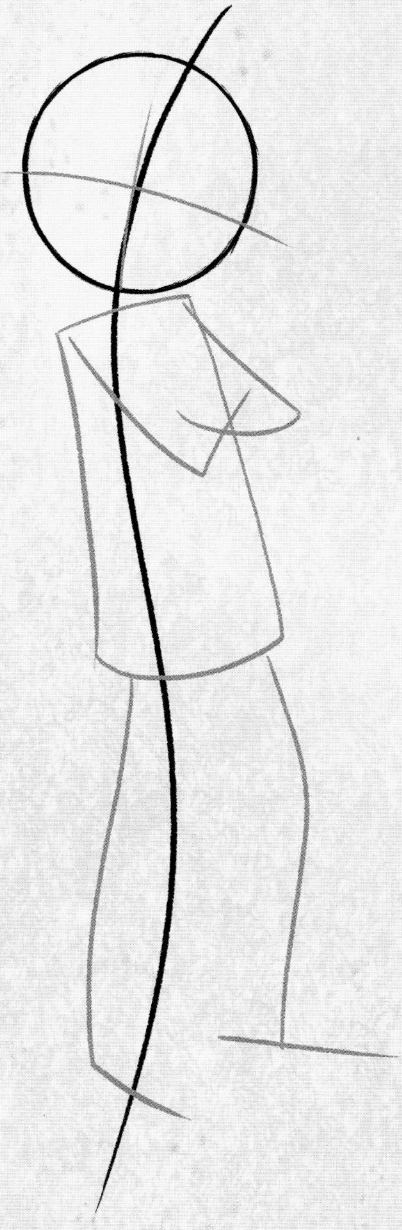

3

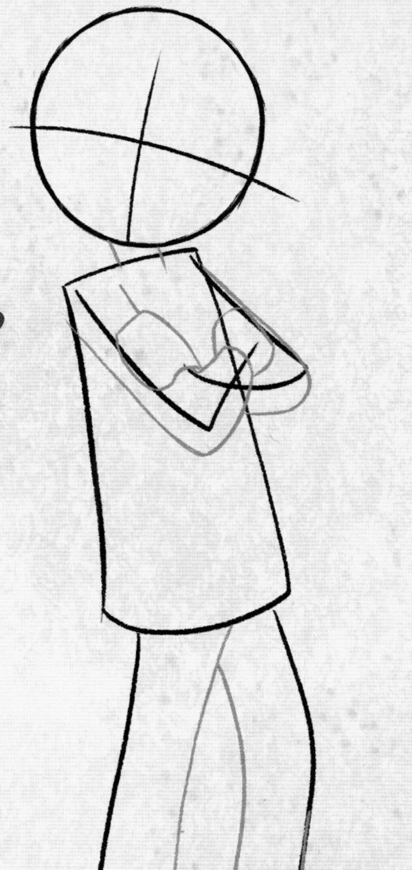

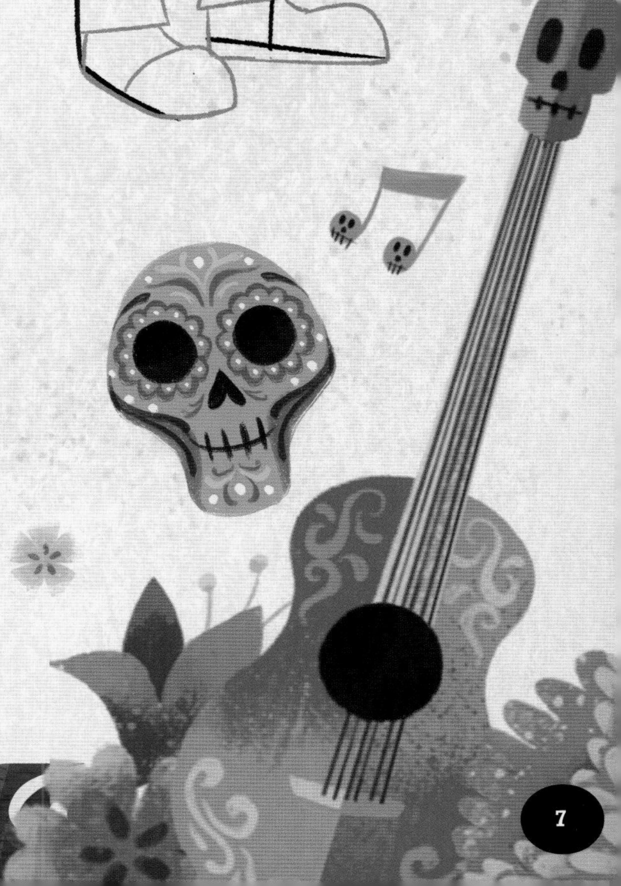

8

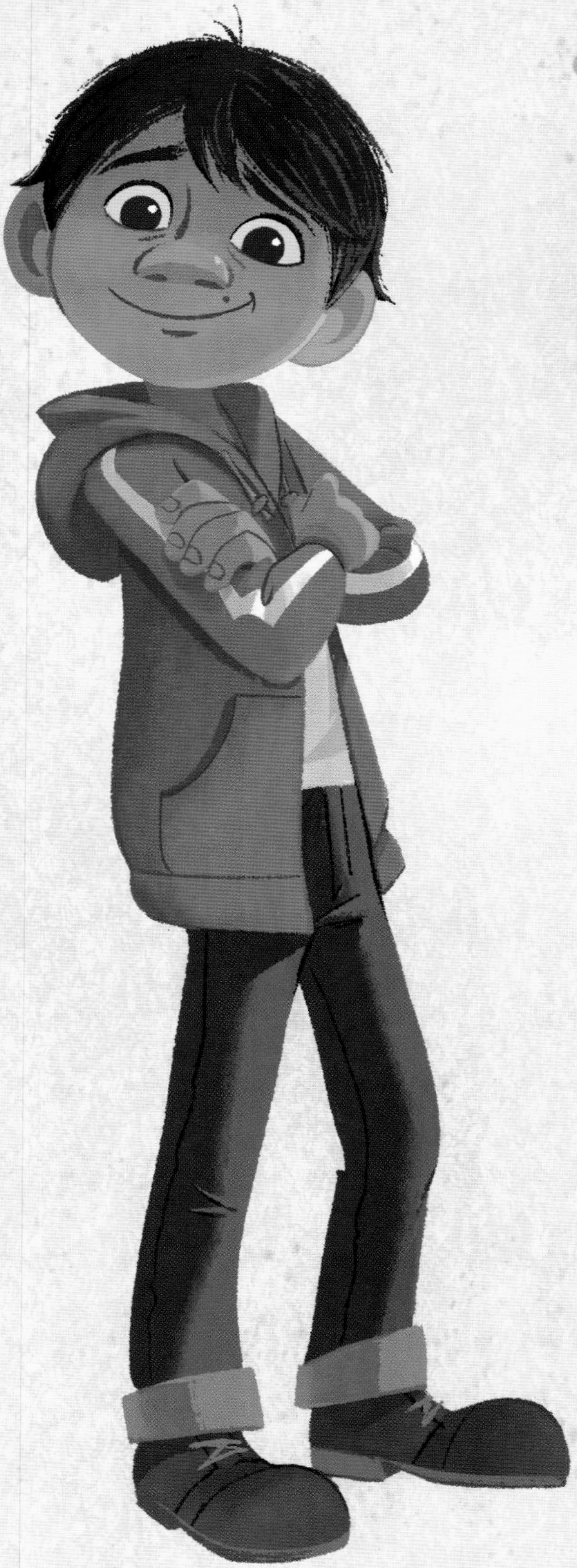

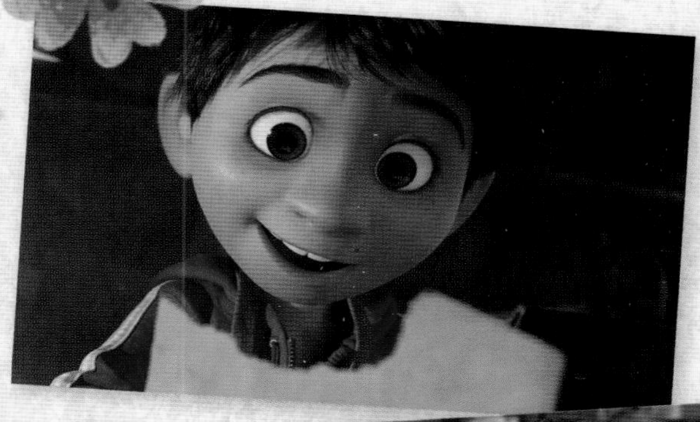

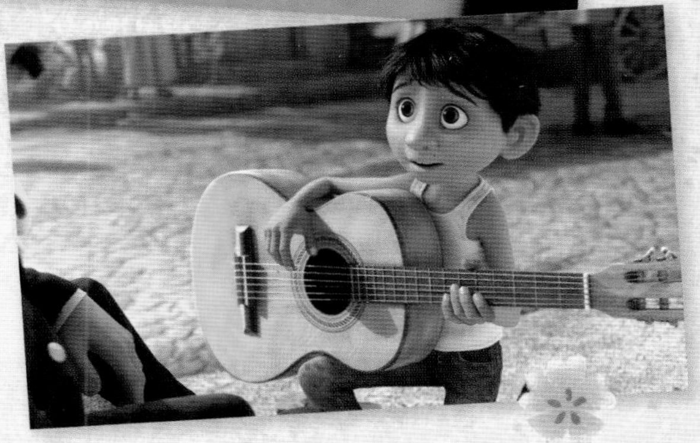

On the eve of Día de los Muertos, Miguel takes Ernesto De La Cruz's guitar from his mausoleum to use in a talent show. He is cursed for stealing from the dead and finds himself stuck in the Land of the Dead. A skeleton named Héctor helps him navigate through this new world, and helps paint Miguel's face with black and white shoe polish so he can blend in. Miguel and Héctor try to get Miguel back home before time runs out.

Coco

Coco, Miguel's cherished great-grandmother, is the only family member who listens to his hopes and dreams. She is very old, fragile, and is losing her memory. The memory of her father is fading from Coco's mind. Miguel sings the song, "Remember Me," to help Coco remember. When she does remember, she decides to reveal her father's identity to the rest of the family.

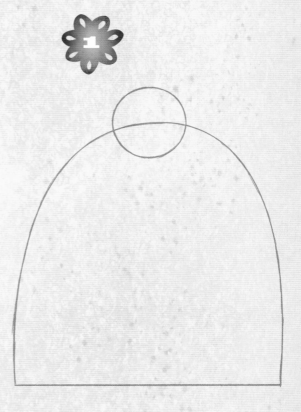

Abuelita

Elena Rivera, known as "Abuelita" to Miguel, is Miguel's grandmother and the ultimate enforcer of the Rivera family's ban on music. She loves her family very much and will do anything to protect them, but when she gets angry, she wields a mean slipper. She pressures Miguel to go into the family's shoe business and ends up destroying his guitar in anger. Abuelita tries to comfort Miguel after doing so, but it doesn't do much good, at least until they make up the next day.

Dante

The goofy, friendly street dog Dante is a hairless Mexican Xoloitzcuintli, or Xolo. He seems to pop up whenever Miguel is near and tags along on Miguel's adventures. When Dante unexpectedly accompanies Miguel on his journey to the Land of the Dead, Miguel begins to see his four-legged friend in a new light: as a spirit guide.

Héctor

Héctor is a scrappy vagrant whom Miguel meets on his journey into the Land of the Dead. Héctor is on the verge of being forgotten, which is a problem because the dead can only survive if they are remembered. To prevent Héctor's "final death," Miguel agrees to keep his memory alive once he returns to the Land of the Living.

Mamá Imelda

Mamá Imelda is the matriarch of the Rivera family and Miguel's great-great-grandmother. In the early 1900s, she started the Rivera family's shoemaking business to support herself and her daughter after her musician husband left home and never returned. While still alive, Imelda decreed that there was to be no music in the Rivera household, an edict that still stands to this day.

Tía Rosita

Tía Rosita is Miguel's late aunt who resides in the Land of the Dead. She is the sister of Miguel's great-grandfather Julio, who was Coco's husband. When Rosita meets Miguel in the Land of the Dead, she knows immediately that he is family. She is so excited to see him that she crashes through Papá Julio and scatters his bones just to hug Miguel.

Tía Victoria

Tía Victoria is Miguel's late aunt who resides in the Land of the Dead. She and Miguel's abuelita were Coco's daughters. Victoria's specialty in the shoe business was huaraches, a type of sandal made from woven leather. When Victoria and Rosita meet Miguel in the Land of the Dead, they realize something isn't quite right with Miguel—he's not dead!

Tío Oscar & Tío Felipe

Tío Oscar and Tío Felipe are Miguel's late identical twin uncles whom he meets in the Land of the Dead. He recognizes them right away because he's seen photos of them. Brothers of Mamá Imelda, they worked in the family's shoe business and were good at their jobs. They can tell Miguel's shoe size just by looking at his footprint!

Pepita

Mamá Imelda's spirit guide is a beautiful but imposing alebrije named Pepita. She looks like a large, colorful jaguar with wings, but when she visits the Land of the Living, she looks like a common house cat. Pepita helps Imelda track down her missing great-great-grandson, Miguel, in the Land of the Dead.

3

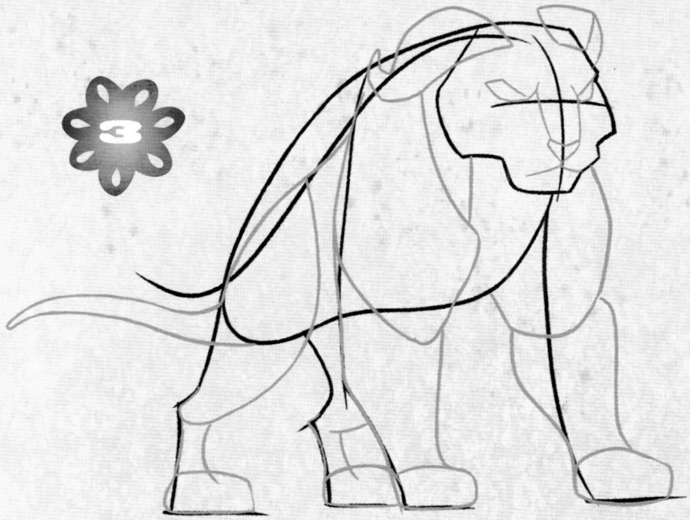

4

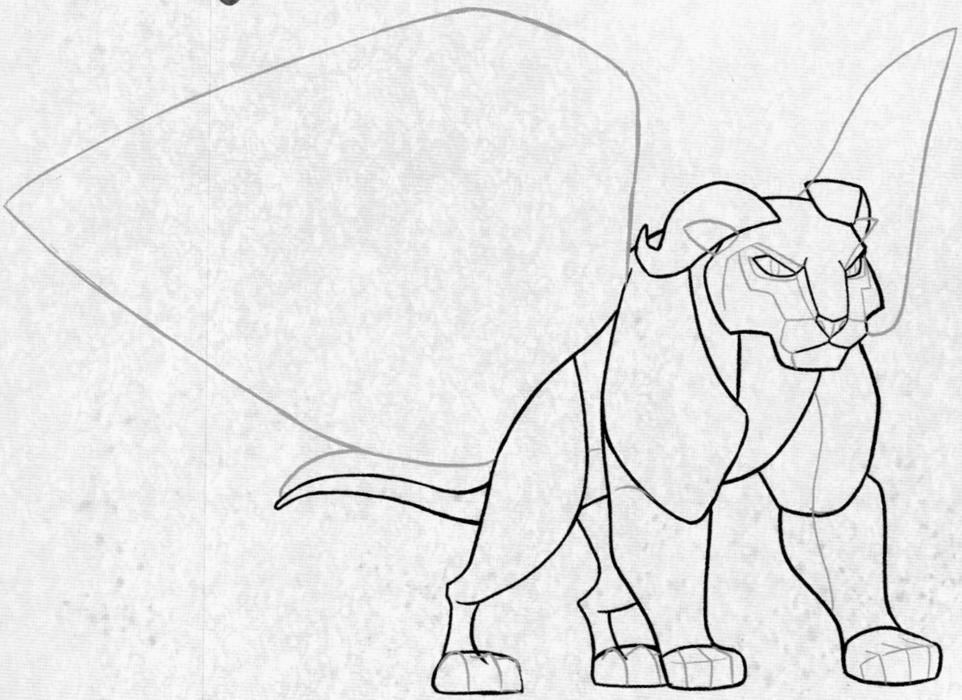

Ernesto De La Cruz

Ernesto De La Cruz is the most famous musician in Mexican history. Star of stage and screen, the charming and charismatic De La Cruz is best known for his hit song "Remember Me." After his tragic death on stage during a live performance, he is now even more beloved in the Land of the Dead than he was in the Land of the Living.

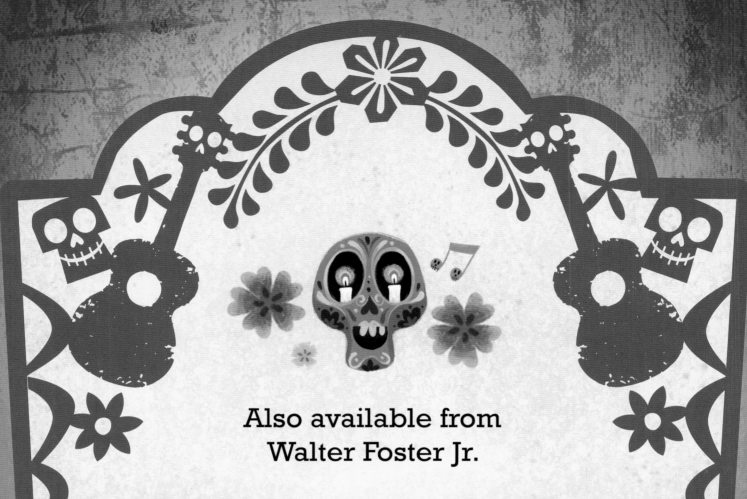

Also available from Walter Foster Jr.

Learn to Draw
Disney•Pixar Cars
ISBN: 978-1-63322-679-1

Learn to Draw
Disney Moana
ISBN: 978-1-63322-144-4

Learn to Draw
Disney Princess
Classic Fairy Tales
ISBN: 978-1-63322-145-1

Visit QuartoKnows.com for more Learn to Draw Disney books.